Being

A Collection of Poems and Haikus for
Life: Embracing Love, Hope, and
Balance

Minal Kering

BookLeaf
Publishing

India | USA | UK

Made with ❤ on the BookLeaf Publishing Platform
www.bookleafpub.in
www.bookleafpub.com

Dedication

This book is for everyone who chooses to follow their dreams and never gives up, against all odds.

Acknowledgement

This book is a testament to the immense gratitude, inspiration, and love I hold in my heart, for each one of you.

To my parents – you are my roots, my foundation, and my guiding light. Everything that I am and what I strive to be is a reflection of your unwavering love and wisdom. I am forever grateful.

To my husband, my partner, my most genuine critic, and my greatest support – thank you for your love, presence, and peace, for your unwavering belief, through life's unpredictable moments.

To my daughters – your curious minds and pure hearts show me new facets of love and life each day. Thank you for this beautiful journey of being your Mum.

To Doc, forever and always, your friendship is home! Thank you for being my person!

To Jo and D, thank you for always being there with your strength, grace, and love, through the laughter and tears of life.

To my great, diverse, and beautiful family, paternal and maternal - thank you for all your love, wisdom, warmth, and belonging.

And to life itself - thank you for being my greatest guru and teacher. These poems and haikus are my way of celebrating this journey.

With heartfelt gratitude,
Minal Kering

Preface

Life flows like a river - ever-changing, unpredictable, yet beautifully profound, in its quiet moments and fierce storms. This collection of poems and haikus is an echo of life, when we pause to truly notice, breathe, and reconnect - with ourselves, and with the world around us.

This collection is to acknowledge the small and big moments in our lives, accompanied by their share of joy and sorrow, triumph and defeat, helplessness and hope.

They remind us to slow down, to listen, and to feel - to truly live.

In your quiet moments of reflection, these poems and haikus will help you find hope, love, and light, to embrace the beauty of the present moment, and the boundless possibilities that lie ahead!

Breathe. Balance. Thrive.

Contents

Mum, What Should I Be?

You can be a baker or a doctor,
An artist, astronaut or a dancer,
Whatever passion and profession you find,
Remember to be compassionate and kind.

Some days may seem sunny and fun,
On others, you simply want to run.
Be honest and strong,
Yet, never side with the wrong.

Be determined and act with grit,
Laugh along and show your wit.
Yet on some days, if you seem to falter,
Be open-minded to be an explorer.

Aim high and reach for the stars,
Follow your path, though the goal may seem
so far.
Have faith and carry on even when you
tumble,

And when you succeed, remember to always
stay humble.

Be generous to others and show them
empathy,
Be loving and patient, with others especially.
Wherever life takes you, whatever your
destiny,
Keep smiling and look up - let that be your
legacy.

Be a pilot and fly high in the skies,
Or be the one who studies the stars.
With all your dreams pursued,
Show some character, show some attitude,
And remember to always express your
gratitude.

Be mindful, be heartful,
And simply be joyful!
Be whatever you want to be,
And at times, when the world seems too fast,
Pause. Breathe. And simply be!

Still in Motion

When life gets you down
You feel lost, stuck, and confused
All may seem stagnant.

Aware that you're down
Growing, learning, and loving
That's when you rise up!

At times, let's choose to
Step back, reflect on what's been
Smile for what's ahead!

Your mind, heart, and soul
Know it's ok to be still
Yet...always moving!

Lost and Found

She missed her new toy
Lost in the park, but found a
New friend to play with.

Didn't clear his exams
Lost a year, but shined in his
True passion for dance!

Lost her innocence
Fear and trauma in her now
Scared to think or feel.

Rise above she did
Empowered and strong, she found
Her inner true self!

They lost the rat race
Missed the promotion and raise
But found their own pace.

With changing times, we
Lose our old relationships,
Have to let them go!

And we find new friends,
Heartful connections anew
For new memories.

You lose love at times
And you find yourself again
Spend time with this self!

Let go of people
You don't need the negative
Relish the peace now!

You lose innocence
Find inner strength to go on
Let's treasure this You!

Keep Walking

Life's a mystery box
With sweet, sour, bitter times
Some good and bad roads!

We all face struggles
Want answers now, won't find them
Only looking back.

Standing where you are
Feel stuck with the same problems
Going in circles.

Look back, then let go
To reach your destination
Walk straight, break the loops!

Sometimes you fall down
Dust off all the dirt and pain
Get up and walk on!

Pain and betrayal
Anger and grief only wind
You up in circles.

Try out the old ways
If you feel like giving up
Tread an untried path.

It's easier said
For paths crooked and scary
Keep on walking straight!

Through its ups and down
Learn and love this life journey
Walk on till the end!

Alone

Days and nights are long,
Don't want to do anything,
Will this ever end?

Staring in the night,
Million thoughts passing me by,
No one to share with!

The world sees colours,
I see only black and white,
Where is the rainbow?

Life has no meaning,
Everything seems blank, want to
Find something to fill.

I've tried it before,
Did not work out very well.
Will I smile again?

Want to try once more,
It's unnerving I know, yet
I'll do this for me.

Forget the past now
Show myself, love and kindness
It is a new day!

Do little, feel good,
Do something more, feel better,
Every single day!

Reach out and connect,
Never know who's listening,
Take that leap of faith!

I'll take the first step,
Talk, connect, empower, heal
Thrive and live again!

Parenthood

Guiding tiny hands
Into responsible ones
Strong, gentle, caring.

Little steps, big dreams
Love them for who they are, not
Their accomplishments.

Listen and unlearn
Be there with your warm presence
Their calm, in chaos.

Parenting is tough
Be kind to yourself and them
Connect, engage, love.

Imperfect, tired
Plentiful hugs, warmth, and laughs
Real parenting!

Balance

With work and home tasks
It's all slog, no play today
No balance they say.

Cooking and school stuff
Days and nights just pile on all
Where's the time to be?

Go on, take a break
And snatch moments in your day
Be with each other.

Play in the garden
See the bright colours around
Sit down and be still.

Smile, go for a walk
Or jump in muddy puddles,
Just giggling away!

Joke, tickle, and hug
Spend time, know each other more
Grans, parents, kids too!

Let's make it happen
Be present with love and joy
Live with balance now!

Unmasked

Popular at school
A talented musician
I cry every night.

Intelligent, cool
A champion sportsperson
No one to talk with!

Should I open up
With my family and friends?
Will they love me still?

Male, female, other,
Gay or straight, I'm a person
I want to unmask!

I'm scared to reveal
My mask is my only shield
Would I be sneered at?

Kind and strong, I am
A best friend and partner too
Just see me for me!

I accept myself
People may take some more time
And that's ok too!

I want to live free
Accepted and included
Just want to be me!

Mindset

Challenges abound
Fear and doubt, but I stand tall
Quiet Mental strength.

Pure and genuine
Focused, steady, impactful
Power of Intent
.

Our voice from within
Or gentle push from others,
A Nudge takes us far.

Take the first step, learn
Fall, fail, and rise up again
Do, make it happen.

Reflect, refocus
Change as you endure and grow
Sustain, this mindset.

Feel the highs and lows
Emotional strength your core
Feel the pounding heart.

Each moment and day
Self, others and universe
Thank you for it all.

Women

She's the best, they say
Mother, Wife, Granny, and friend
It's "her", they forget!

The roots holding fort
Silently strong, yet graceful
Always there for you.

She gives and she bears
Creates, nurtures, and protects
Leaves herself behind.

She has goals and dreams
Her purpose awaiting glow
It's her time to shine.

Passion in her heart
She treads slowly but surely
Carving her own path.

Strong, kind, inspiring
She binds everyone along
Yes, she's a woman!

It's Your Way

Try new and old ways
If you feel like giving up
Tread an untried path.

It's not easy though
For paths untouched and unseen
Remind yourself why!

Why does it matter?
Focus at the heart of it
Walk, the way appears!

Fail and then succeed
Celebrate small and big wins
It's all emotions.

Be inspired, yet
Compare yourself to no one
Be free to be you!

Through its ups and downs
Learn to love your life journey
Walk at your own pace.

Be kind to yourself
Realistic, consistent
Walk on your own way!

The Journey of Pain

No one asks for pain
It sure can be life-changing
All may seem hopeless.

Tales of what could be
Echoes of lost memories
Flowing down in tears.

Be it physical
Mental, emotional pain
Changes shape in time.

Learn to rise again
Pain can never define you
Keep moving forward.

Dig deep inside you
Find your strength, fire to fight
Make pain your power!

Purpose

What makes your soul sing
Mind and heart work together
That's your true **Passion**.

What, where, who and when
Is this truly what I want
Understand deeply.

Troubles may creep in
Dig deep and make a **Resolve**
Commit with courage.

Won't be a smooth ride
Show grit and be **Persistent**
Remind yourself why.

Pause, look back, reflect
Open-minded, critical
Re-align your path.

Know your Ikigai
Listen to what your heart says
Seek **Satisfaction**.

Look out for others
Connect with community
Everyone along.

Find, re-find purpose
Embrace and work towards it,
Act, make it happen.

Love what you do, and
Give back to others, truly
Mindfully heartful!

Music

Music is freedom
Connects across languages
Pure and complete joy.

When I'm lost or stuck
Music is my therapy
Through the highs and lows.

A breath of fresh air
The quiet embrace needed
Music is heartful.

No words and no rules
It's the sound of what I feel
Travels through my soul.

My peace in chaos
Brings me closer to myself
Music is power.

Melodies, rhythms
Music is the symphony
Harmony of life.

Friendship

Thirty years ago
We first met as teenagers
Diverse as can be.

Something clicked, felt right
And just like that, we became
The bestest of friends!

Quirky and crazy
We found so much in common
Our dreams and our goals.

Bike rides and night outs
College years went by, you are
Friend, family, home!

Thousand miles way
Twenty years, marriage, jobs, kids
Birthday wishes done.

Yearly life updates
Distance, silence and our lives
Went quietly by.

One day a message
Time and distance didn't matter
Been right here, always!

In difficult times
Our friendship becomes our strength
Keeps us moving on.

We cry and we laugh
And we can be our true selves
That's what real friends are!

A friendship like this
Time tested through ups and downs
Rare and hard to find.

Joy and happiness
Cheering on for each other
Makes life meaningful.

Grateful for you friend
Unconditionally so
You are my person!

Run Smarter

A typical day
Making meals, packing lunches,
Rush to work and school.

Busy daily lives
Drop-offs and pick-ups galore
Chores, kids and work tasks.

Fast-paced weeks endless
Days and nights seem like a blur
Do it all again.

Ticking tasks and goals
We're all just running along
Ready for the next.

Days and years go by
Those who matter, merely are
A beautiful blur!

So out of breath now
When did we last smile and laugh
Missing a warm hug.

Call on a dear friend
Pause and notice something new
Take a moment, breathe.

Work, chores, goals and dreams
Home shoes, work shoes, parent shoes
Can't just run away.

Let's change how we run
Sing, dance, love, smile, thank some more
Let's all run smarter!

Mindfully savour
Heartfully appreciate
Treasure this new run!

Beauty

They say beauty is flawless
Perfect skin, hair, and makeup no less.
Isn't beauty something more
Engrained in our every pore.

Dark circles and tired eyes
A parent's love never lies.
Wrinkled faces and grey hair
Oh, what beauty in tender care.

Shiny masks a mere cliche
Hiding the trials of everyday.
Are you good enough?
It's all mind stuff.

What you see in the mirror
Is that you or just a blur?
Find yourself through your eyes
Bold, beautiful, and wise.

Embrace who you are
Your strength will take you far.
Believe in yourself

Isn't that beauty in itself?

Curious, kind, with grace
Compassionate, and a smiling face.
With pure intent and heart
You're a world apart!

Won't find it in a mirror's reflection
It's in your words of affection.
This beauty, soaked in your core
A strong yet quiet roar.

Beauty is what's inside
Love, joy, and pride.
It's your own radiant canvas
Of profound soulful bliss!

Values Forever

Fear, angst, doubt galore
Showing up with silent grace
Courage, to go on.

Kindness is simple
A look, touch, act – worth so much
Sprinkle it around.

Deep wounds scar the soul
Find peace, and let yourself heal
Forgive, to be free.

Whispers in your heart
Tomorrow is a new day
Hope is forever.

Big moments and small
Cherish them, make memories
Gratitude for all!

Breathe

Breathe, slow and easy
Inhale, positive and light
Exhale qualms away.

Each and every breath
A precious gift to do more
Make the most of it!

Breathe soft, and reflect
No matter what, you are strong
Know, you are ok.

It's in your control
Every breath is a new chance
Here and now for sure.

Breathe, you are enough
This moment is what matters
Life is calling you!

Breathe, it's a new day
Mind, body, soul together
Gratitude to life!

Silence

Silence is soft, yet so loud
It drowns out the crowd.
The quiet hum of grit
It helps us endure, and commit.

Words can sometimes deceive
Stories make us disbelieve.
Silence brings us closer to reality
It makes us feel free!

Dancing thoughts in the mind
How it yearns to unwind.
Seek out those hushed spaces
Clarity and simplicity in silent places.

It's the sound of grief, through tears
Silence scatters our deepest fears.
The language of pure and true love
It's the highest form of self-love.

Silence is profound and deep
The loudest we can speak.
Silence can be our power,

Our hearts and minds, to empower!

Choose your peace and control
The pathway to your soul.
Silence is our last breath
In the peaceful trumpets of death!

Flow Happy

Just like a river
Life is constant, in its change
Moves and streams along.

Adjust, sustain, grow
Find a way around or through
Into the unknown.

Sad, angry, unsure
Feel, let go in your own time
Know, this too shall pass.

Don't chase happiness
Create experiences
Deep and meaningful.

What makes us happy?
Friends, nature, art, music, sports
Engage, immerse, thrive!

Be kind to yourself
Compassionate to others
Gratitude and joy.

Find your true purpose
Enriching relationships
Mindfully heartful!

Laughter, love, and care,
In moments and memories
Happiness lives here.

Make it a life choice
Not the end, but the journey
Flow along, happy!

www.ingramcontent.com/pod-product-compliance
Lightning Source LLC
Chambersburg PA
CBHW061725130726

47996CB00006B/2497